D1491172

I ♥ YOUR FATE

ANTHONY MCCANN

I ♥ YOUR FATE

WAVE BOOKS   SEATTLE/NEW YORK

Published by Wave Books

www.wavepoetry.com

Wave Books titles are distributed to the trade by
Consortium Book Sales and Distribution
Phone: 800-283-3572 / SAN 631-760X

This title is also available in a limited edition
directly from the publisher

Library of Congress Cataloging-in-Publication Data
McCann, Anthony.
I heart your fate / Anthony McCann. — 1st ed.
p. cm.
ISBN 978-1-933517-51-3
I. Title.
PS3613.C3453113 2011
811'.6—dc22
2010034254

Designed and composed by Quemadura
Printed in the United States of America

9 8 7 6 5 4 3 2 1

FIRST EDITION

Wave Books 027

1. THE EVENT

2. I ♥ YOUR FATE

3. NEW DREAMS OF
MAMMAL ISLAND

1

THE EVENT

POST FUTURISM

1

When I was young, life
was instrumental and
through experience (in life)
(through which I poured myself)
I passed through various
Containers of
pre-dawn excellence.
I remember saying something (once)
on the rooftop just at dawn, something
softly to my hands, when
through the slender wind-bent birch
I spied the new researchers—
all their eyes pressed shut—
from multiple perspectives.
And soon we praised the roof together,
measured weather with our skins.

2

In imitation of their songs
it's now softly I begin
speaking to my hands
where Tiny Futurism sleeps.
I remember saying something like
"slender wind-bent birch."
As tiny broken Mayakovsky
re-expired in my palm
the city's wild, northern rooms
filled with piercing light
like sterilized Containers
of Brooding Arctic Milk.
Good Silver Doves
in whirling squads
plunged into the roar
while out beyond
Dawn's swayback
hills   pale windows
paved the void.

3

And on the Airport Bus,
the 6:10 or 6:03, I read
over your shoulder how
There Is No Futurism.

4

But what I said about all this,
repeating what you'd read and
re-reading what I'd read and
all we thought was said,
was all erased, or most of it,
with magnets, while I slept
on the benches at Gate Six.

But I might remember something said
it later seemed to me, like

"sterile arctic rooms," or
"blue-yellow wind-bent eyes."

So here I'll stay, enchanted,
in the pulsing terminal, watching
clouds in mirrored pillars
dream their shadows on the tile

OMOA (TIME OF THE GRACKLE)

I soon perceived this wild coast—
     real, yet unborn—
to be
     bastilled by

at every side
a boundless waste of rocks.

In this boasted land of freedom,
     generally speaking,
the cruelty of presence
shall never be sufficient.

Most of the poor fish in boats and
fish is their principal food.

Each night falls like ashes alone
on their socks

in a room
by the stair.

But how dangerous to foster these feelings!
This, indeed, is the world.

To my right: a bird. To my left:
a bird. Such are the thoughts
of all the birds:

"Oh how food kills us all and
every seat is dark
with superhuman stains."

Wormy, bearded and
raging at the dirt
the last, late bus approaches.

And so, slick with aftergrease,
we reach a place
where each
is given names.
The same
       bare bulb
dangles

in the shack of the police as
Dusk, sleepwalking,
leaks up through all the terms.

Any sound
that falls now
from your mouth·
becomes land or
food for birds.

OF THE MOCKINGBIRD

The purpose of behavior is disputed.
Though it serves
a hopped display

hammered in distinctness

from high points
in the distance

or summoned
at our homes.
They uncork their
wingèd heraldry
to pop
across the wires:
the whole regal and bionic
jingle of the world.
I'm speaking of the mockingbird.

The sky is something else: a mirror
that advances

The television on, everyone advancing

Up Third to Virgil, down Virgil
to Sixth, past Lafayette Park, up
Lafayette Park,
left on
Third, back
to Alexandria where
I stop and eat a bowl of
frozen eyes

Delicious but too fast

So that once again, belovèd readers,
I find that I have died. I die
each time inside my body
each time I eat your food—
O World
(By which I always mean THE LIGHT)

Or let's just say
there's a forehead
between my body and the light
and it deactivates the World

This presentation is over. Now
I'm just driving around

FIELD WORK

Later, on the ridge, in samurai dress
I appear. It's me. In mustache. And gear.

The moat is full of
CHERRYBLOSSOMS and I count
the cries of
BIRDS. Beyond that moat is
TEENAGE FRANCE. There youths frolic,
pace and

resemble me. But
what kind of person
is a person

like this? My fingers
put shadows
on all of the
birds

as just
beyond song
birds
scrape up the sky.

We ride
       on a haycart
down through
their codes. In the village

the villagers
dress
in blue codes. Our fathers

make shadows
all over their
caps. I mean

our fingers
make shadows
on the faces
of cops. We cross the

late bridge
to our fathers.

THE ASSISTANT

There's a need to
return to decorum—
discipline, silence and
hugs. This need
is not felt by the
TRUMPETER swan, clattering now
onto land
chased by the
flannel researchers, slashing now
through the pond.
      Crouching
here
     in the moss

         they smell
sweet and
sour
as rain—   woolly
    rain

on
rubber hats
on
woolly hats
and tweed.
My investment

in melancholy
is both
great and sufficient
in these
sweet
rubber
people
and hats.
And I know
that beyond these

PLANET SIZED CLOUDS
there'll be a

gray and blue cloud

so I don't
use my knees

to press on
through my body
out
through the window
to sound

Later we saw
EAGLES
we saw
eagles
big as nouns

DRAGA BARBARA,

What kind of lamp is this lamp that I see?
It looks like a fried horse with sticks or a
piece of flatbread
    wrapped
on a moon.
Frankly I don't understand
this fleet of little felt squares
under each leg of each
table and chair
but I guess the wood here is soft.
Now the weather is
more
hot than soft
and I wonder what all your things mean:
the clown in the room to the left and
this jug
in the room to the right—
it looks like a clown,
a robot clown,

in a red coat
with plugs
and no heads. When your father invented
invisible shoes
when he overproduced
the invisible shoes
where here did he
store the remainders? I drank six beers
in your house today, Barbara,
and threw out all the bottles
downstairs so you wouldn't know
what you already know.
How can one person
have so many soaps? Who is this little
crab girl
with the mermaid tail
in the dish?
So many soaps and still my feet stink.
I think all your neighbors must love you
because you're so tall and funny and kind.
So when we talk on the phone
why can't I confess
that though I like H and M
I still want my clothes back.
Tell Misha I love him back too.

Truth is, Barbara, I don't know how to begin
to touch the terrible truth.
To touch the thing with my feet:
The truth of my shoes, Barbara,
how they sit here alone
how they squat in your room how they reek
how they stink like two really dead squirrels
and *you* so concerned with *your* mess.

PUTIN WITH LYNCH

In the world the dwellings are all made of wood
And every house is a beautiful ship
But there's a parallel world attached to this world
Which are these paths drawn thinly down through the woods
And I meet you there now under the bridge
Where we hear the snow sing snow songs to itself
And then somehow we're just sledding away!
Totally free like the songs that we sing
As the sled sings the song of a sled to the snow
But there's a parallel world there under the snow
Of crinkling earth and little green leaves
Of grass struggle tips pushing up through the snow
The grass thinking snow thinking snow thinking snow
And under the grass the system of roots
The systemless system of dark wiggle roots
And the master who lurks in the rooms after dark
In his motionless hand the luminous milk

POEM

cleaning what we took to be a field
was really just a foldout bed full of crumbs
the boozy Czechs all gentle friendship and touching
were just further proof this life is a dream
you see I was reading the Complete Poverty of X
in the Accidental Library of Like Total Self Neglect:
all these weird ex-boxers on the backyard couch
and then the weeds go and grow up through everything
the ailanthus stutters over the cracks
and you go and do your "Badger Stomp"
as if we'd ever seen a badger outside of a John Clare poem
but let us stomp together before the underthings of leaves
and after a long day of modeling "life skills" to the poor
under The Poor Aren't Poor They're Ignorant Initiative
it's as if, as it were, I were actually piloting this blood
as the train slides out of the bucketed land
and I swing my gaze over the crumpled land

over the bodies of strangers looking for eyes
it wasn't me that asked me to come here
but then they drifted off into their symptoms
while I handed out my symptoms
and these years turned into rooms

LETTERS OF CLAIRE AND TRELAWNY

1

With my cocaine shovel
I dig up emotions

In the moon
My shovel

Sparkles like words

White beautiful words
With names like "Cocaine"

(I kiss each word
On its beautiful name)

But you're late, my shovel
Says to the dirt

You're late, he says
To my feelings

So digging and digging
I smash up my shovel

On the blue ice
Skullcap of the moon

"Great Events! Great Events!
But my habits!"
I write

"How shall I tell you!
Do you not know?"

And you, in your boots
In the secondhand snow,

Threadbare boots
In the moon-shattered snow,

This is what you write in return

2

You have guessed I should
Discover the reason
My heart shuts up
At every approach

I possess so many friends
It seems to throw gloom
On the shadows and grease
Of their wild crusades

I climb a few more
Wet sprockets of Moscow
To this balcony over
The unbuttoned lights

All the buildings are thinking
What's wrong with that bitch
As I drool from the balcony
Down into my life

Down in my life
The Russians are snoring
A sweet song about laundry
Called "I Fall Apart"

I'm down in my life
With your name in my face
With sorrow I think
Of my pockets and hands

SAMUEL TAYLOR COLERIDGE

I want to lie on the slope
I wish to lay in the shade
on top of a hill, in bald California
under a spreading blue tree

and through my brassy spyglass
I will watch the city advance
the contracts, the workers, contractors
the plywood, and dust buttered trucks

I will dream of rivers of glue
I will roll to the right to the left
I'll fondle the world in the grass
and shout at the birds and the planes

tiny workers in tiny work suits
the workers in white worker suits
the workers in grimy T-shirts
then I'll trundle back through tall grass

tall swaying tawny thin grass
rhyming my steps with my words
the sea will appear, pocked with sails
Then I'll enter your life

DEAR CATHOLIC CHURCH,

Just once in my life
I want to see a real gargoyle
eat a live human soul
like a peach
from a bowl of cream
which is to say
I want to see a live
human gargoyle
eat a peach
from a world bowl of
suffering
and in this way
I will never be your man

Which is to say
I was built by hand
in the previous century
by dockworkers
immigrants all

I am the one true church
the confusing thing is
outside it's different

Which is to say
I was built by hand
by a live human gargoyle
they call me Peaches

I mean it's sunny
and medieval
and fake in the world
and between the idea of food
and the abomination of the lampposts
I am the middle term
call me Food

Which is to say
I have chosen this love
I was chosen
by my choice

Dear Catholic Church
I forbid you

THE EVENT

I came to describe the animal
But the animal was alive
The animal was unnamed
And the animal

Was always moving

I came here to describe the animal
But all these shoes stood in my way

Shiny black dress shoes
Elegant leather sandals
Brilliant lacquered nails

I must have been down on my knees again
Following the animal

I came here to describe the animal!
I'm shouting

Struggling to my feet
Where did this cocktail party come from?

When did all these
Aristocrats
     get here?

I whimpered

Brushing the dust
From my knees

Which is when I saw you

     dirt
         eyes
             sloppy
       pink
  laughing
     dust
         in your hair

I knew you'd come
To describe the animal
And I never drank again

2

I ♥ YOUR FATE

I came out of the past, with fingers all stained
Behind my face my brain glows like carp
It's like this, you'll see, even in pictures
Leave it to someone to figure that out

That sad bug guy just imitates birds
Hey guy, I said, hailing the dude
The flowers you gave me weighed like ten pounds
But I walk up that hill every night

Still, I won't put the moon in my poem
The moon knocks at the window, each window it makes
These bugs deposit some eggs in the dust
I respect the impulse, but can't understand

The weather was there, a feeling like teeth
A small kindness, something like that
She'd wanted to listen to my voice late at night
She'd asked me to mail my voice to her home

I'd only wanted to speak truth to weather
It doesn't *matter*, it's going to *happen*
The moment withered, stood up and looked
I leaned in to get kissed, but I'd misunderstood

*

Here's something as thoughtful as chairs in the snow:
Blue socks piled up under trees in the snow
This place is named for a less-recent place
One day I walked in and sat down at the bar

I raised my dumb flag over drab painted land
Merciful, purple, my night hammer reeked
Hair grew from my bottle, cracked in the snow
Like hatpins in corners where tooth-rabbits lurk

This world: so crowded with me-ghosts of me
"Historical Thoughts" or "Blue Dukes in the Snow"
I leaned into the phone—I listened for votes!
The snow in the dark humming like rails

The night is air travel—my heart seen from space
Dead car in the snow, stuffed with old brooms
Each now is a dot, a sentence—in place
I stack up my feelings like table-free rags

Tossing chairs from the roof—the snow in my hair
Or asleep in the tree in my little boy suit
Man-sized birds passed over the barn
So I crossed out the moon, the trees, and the barn

*

A man on blue shoulders drifts through white lights
I followed these words from the bar to your face
Keep talking, I said, to my wrist and my thumb
Can't think of my friends without joy and new shame

I like the chapter where Karl gets fired
Let's waste the whole day feeling these things
From up where he lived I could see tiny mouths
He sat in the tub, white sun on his hands

Behind my vision I'm flattened and blank
I know now what will happen, it's perfectly clear
From the balcony lips I watch your mistake
My lungs are content, but the liver is blind

One imitates wind between stars with a mouth
I sat on the carpet, white socks on my hands
In the book I was reading: door after door
Falling through cotton, I landed in dimes

The face on display slowly opened its eyes
Little gold bird, don't ask me your name
You're right there inside, but I'll text you from here
Together we fluttered, mentoring tears

*

Can organized body hair still be alive?
In what forms can the ants be said to believe?
I'm up late at night just to curse at the ants
I went out on the roof: the city looked stern

You lie in the dark: I'll make up a name
It's not a profession—it's more like a word
The moon hobbles up over cruddy old boots
We fucked on the roof, not everyone looked

The cat burrowed into me reading its nails
I'd wandered all night in the forest of props
Two shoes on a curb always mean something strange
I can drive, with eyes closed, for 38 years

The moment had come—why did I sit?
Mongols need Laws! I typed into my phone
We've all stared, forlorn, at a disemboweled couch
This fantasy scene's called the Real Farewell

In the Secret Farewell I was licking your eyes
Dreamy, ironic: the moon shopped for roots
In the dark a body can find its true form
I can dive, using body noise, right through a door

*

You came in from the street riding your thoughts
There—that one's me—don't call it a couch
Put on these pants, today you're the plan
We don't get together to make you feel bad

To examine these feelings I get up and leave
Thing about him, dude gets off a phone
Took me two hours just saying goodbye
I was happy for you, but nobody cared

When I talk about writing mostly I lie
"Timberly" means like one or two things
This forest smells like really old cars
I describe my own body with unlikely clouds

Regarding your letter, loose dread licked my bones
I couldn't remember your name and my mom's
I misspoke her name till I thought of my mom
Each of our habits now points to a star

Grey-bellied and low—both soundless and far
Something incredible's wrong with this dance
First goes the liver, as goes the face
Clutching your hip, I stutter and gasp

*

Music came back and made us its slave
It's not clear just yet how much I recall
I kept licking your wrist as if I had knees
I don't know if this is like reading your mind

Shame requires a theory of mind
A sequence of numbers lies under the skin
There's a system of noise just under your skin
In each sentence lurks a sacred command

I finger your pendant like jewelry was real
Tall shadows of clouds sleep on these hills
A sentence of death hides in every command
I push through these feelings, past music, to sound

In all music lurks a simple command
I struggle to locate your voice on my skin
Think with your body, smash with your mind
"Now, right now," you said, biting your friend

I want to be there when that music begins
Music, come back—make us your slave
Tiny hands move just under the skin
Stay with this feeling, right here, where it ends

WERTHER

All Sunday I lay in the woods in great pain
(I address thus the unseen watching me now)
This is the law by which weaklings are governed:
Twinkle of bird flesh and wind-crinkled leaves

In a site prepared by the dead for our joy
I lay in the grass with the beetles and worms
To watch the light count off each little blade
Breathing in dirt smell, sky smell and noise

Oh to roll on the grass with my feelings and hands!
For this is how the tiny words work
Had I only my mouth I would not even bite
And shine on like money shines over a void

It's almost as if I were saying these things
To someone—to you—or not even to you
You stood—like the day—by the bench—with your bag
While the birds and the traffic referred to themselves

I'd passed through this pain to a new kind of strange
(How perfect it is to believe in the sad)
I count all the teeth on your feet with my teeth
With distance I measure your silence to mean

*

We captured their leader and cut off his head
They gang-raped the dude and then cut off his head
What makes you think I care what you think
I don't have a body to feel afraid

I want to be there at the end of the state
I'm afraid to be here at the end of the state
Tall shadows of rain dream over the hills
The radio tower leaks on through the mist

There is no word for this pain in my breast
Describing your poem I burst into tears
We're drinking blue drinks, on the porch, with the birds
I'm pretty much glad to be gone from this world

All this sun, my heart is a toad
We assembled ourselves in threes round a song
Our blood is still bright, we're lighter than rocks!
A mile below you I'm wired for sound

Soft moccasin light streams down through the leaves
Can't live a day in a world without birds!
I drag myself toward you using only my face
To see each little flower, forever, at once

DESERET

Here's a whole lake—infected with wind
Miles and miles of salt and then sound
While all this time the highway poured toward me
Bringing you and the promise of words

In my head I point to the world with my voice
It's raining down there—but up here there's sun
On the plane, through the window, the sun on your throat
It's me that rattles inside of the hull

A tongue in my head, between teeth, on your eye
To listen for you I lean back in my skull
The desert there breathing: dun table of lumps
First close your eyes—then keep me in mind

Light fills the eyes of the dead generations
A bright plate of meat on a cold metal chair
I put on my robes again, fingering light
Like this at the window: the road and the land

It was their generation, followed by yours
Marbles pouring across wooden floors
Enormous windows filled with bright noise
Light in the marbles, trapped in the flaws

*

I had to go back and touch the stove twice
There was shit on the stoop, I had to go back
We all know the world is encoded with dreams
When touching the world be merry or grave

Footsteps on pavement: white voices, no words
You came up behind me while I pictured the scene
I fear this next line could cause my own death
The hand is still moving as the curtain descends

This world-ridding, path-clearing logic is pain
I drift past these punks out into the lights
Let's add some flute here and mumble beneath
There are 3 or 4 songs I like better than friends

It's rare that I'm able to enjoy time with friends
Keep talking, I said, to my wrist and my thumb
Called you up—(in my head)—"I want my soul back!"
Sometimes my thoughts leak out through my brains

I slowed down the film to watch your hair breathe
We imagined ourselves both noble and sad
In the future all of these horses are blind
They wear hoods to protect our eyes from the flies

*

The surface is quiet; I'm suffering joy
Silently weeping she sniffed at my hair
All the blood, together, spilled from my face
May happy precision inflect your whole fate

"What have you done?" our someone exclaimed
You shrieked as though you'd stabbed me yourself
It was weird: being there, with the rocks and the trees
I leapt from the platform into your arms

You gazed down through the branches, the flowers, to me
I saw myself stumble from two miles out
When I opened the door you leapt into my arms
All the water spilled from my body at once

I was happy, adrift, in the spectacle fires
When I opened my mouth little bodies came out
In my dream there were dogs, blue feathers and dread
The cops filmed our wounds while we strolled in the park

As the city acquired a specialty light
As each night we watched the light drain from its wound
I can't really imagine what anything's like
But at times I'm compelled to recall how I felt

*

In this forest milieu: an encounter with void
I burst from the scrub to the roar of the crowd
Was a horse, untethered, alone in the glade
I stood in your place while you backed away

A horse is some kind of encounter with legs
The enormous head, hooded, just lowered itself
Here is precisely what gentleness is
There was shit on the stairs, I had to go back

Oh to wiggle and still be blessed and have legs!
Now here is a landscape for feeling bald things
This path wanders down through some unfurnished thoughts
I followed these ruts to your shack in the pines

O little blue bird, clear voice of the pines
Your letter has made me hot with new joy
Truly I tremble here in my plight
To have passed this close to one animal's health!

I dozed with my view of the stream and the hills
Woke with blue fur in my teeth and my beard
Slowly—in bloom—my skull grew new eyes
Thin-fingered light slipped down through the pines

*

The clouds drifted over a late human lunch
From miles away the tiny clouds came
Soft moss underfoot, far-off rage of the dogs
Protect me, my love, from these horrible words

When the rains began I was waiting for you
The sky opened up and delivered this sound
It makes my lips linger here near the plates
Each thing we perform is rehearsing for death

This miracle gland gives my body no rest
To be emptied again by the meaningless roar
Let's go die, and then die, and then die and then die
Roll on, little toes, to the top of the earth!

I address this next line to the mind of the trees
The trees are green hair, all wild and ripped
Then the world slumps and is soft as clay heads
I lie at your feet and imagine my eyes

The hedge behind me is filled with small eyes
Each animal seems like a personal trait
All of these signs—but only one word!
Demented! Demented! I run through the woods

*

It's strange to be seen, I've said to a tree
To have trembled so much while breathing the air
For I stood by the lake and was taking its place
And you were the first to see me be seen

You sat and I watched you watching me watch
I was hearing the wind and then seeing the wind
I'd slowed down the film to watch your hair seethe
So that you were The Phantom and I was The Hand

I'm over your face—leaning in—to your face
(I watch the light change as your eyes re-adjust)
Soft lids close over the voice in its dream
Cloud shadows drift and shoot over the lake

Vacant and bright I hoist breakfast flags
Just watching the lake I'm forgetting your face
Hot, wet and alive—slickened with beads
All I see is your tongue, where it sits, in your head

No object here aches to be seen (except me)
Once again I'd arrived at the limit of friends
It might just be me and it might not be me
But it's nice to be held while watching the waves

3

NEW DREAMS OF

MAMMAL ISLAND

YOUR VOICE

But one day they changed the color of everything
It was kind of like tasting all the world's locks
And then a girder the size and shape of a fork
Fell to the floor and presented this room
And a bus barreled down and the whole building quaked
And the trees opened their shirts stepped out of their shirts
Out of their pants stepped out of their pants
And the trees started to weep I mean rain it was raining
And stood there all naked and human and shaking
And your face was an image of waiting in that rain
A kind of rain smeared face half irritation half despair
The despair having given way to a blank detachment
Which itself had given way to a kind of illumination
And this illumination shone through now as post animal joy
So to speak with you was confusing always at best
Unless I looked at your shoes or away at the distance
And never locked eyes, never looked at your face

DREAMS OF WAKING

Over the photographed earth to the photographed park
Once I woke up in my ape suit "just thinking"
It was very important to be prevalent once
Extreme States was just the name of my shirt
And to hegemonize sleep was not just a game
With the drool of a year attached to my name
My left eye still smeared happily shut
Napping means to go drool shadow now
While the sky scalds itself with aluminum dread
Back in nineteen whatever you fill in the blank
Can you believe now once how my body talked
With all these words in the hands of the dead
Every day I disown myself twice wake again
Go back to sleep with my brains in my hands

ALIBI

When the rains began
I was raining
When the road began I was looking
When you arrived
I was linking
In the body sauce
I was steeping
Then I was walking
Then I was wailing
Scratching my scalp
Erasing
Erasing
When the bus arrived
I was waiting
Pursed on the hill
When the woods spoke
I was sleeping
in the crinkle moss

When the roots talked
I was sleeping
in the crinkle moss
When the city honked
I was honking
When the building loomed
I was lurking
in the shadow
by the building tree
When the urine stank
I was sniffing
near the building tree
by the urine pool
When the people talked
I was holding together
When I opened the fridge:
Leprosy Tanks!
I'm up on the ladder
when the leaves start to shake
I am holding my hair
holding my teeth
I am resembling knees
when the birds start to twitch
In the meantime:

Miracle Cops!
Filled with small traits
I was combing my head
When you touched my wrist
I was leaning

LETTER NEVER SENT

The hills in the yellowing light
The sound of traffic far off
I remember the names of the grass
The terrible names of each blade

The sound of my voice in your name
To memorize you and your hands
Your lips, how they close when you look
How you looked repeating my name

Oh, please just no more events!
To kiss all your noise and your name
Now I describe my emotions
The sky is a lowercase x

I say the names of my hands
First left and then right and then right
Strange to have hands and a name
I look down to my hands when I speak

I don't say my name to my hands
(I'll save that dark magic for last!)
This event will go unrecorded
Weird, fake birds overhead

IN THE VISITORS' LOCKER ROOM

Now imagine the vagina
Picture the unfolding of the
Buttery vulva

Picture the swollen wrinkly lips
The shiny pulsing clit

And then picture the world

A parking lot
In the desert

Wind
The rumble and rattle of traffic
The day's last light
Darkness settling
Over the pumps

You are a traveler
You are entering
The glass cube
Of this Chevron station

Your hand is on the door handle
You are pulling open the door
The little bell is jingling

And you remember nothing else
Not where you are from
Nor where you are going

So that this wonderful vagina
Has become even more appealing

And you can touch it with your nose
And you can wiggle your nose in it
And then you can kiss it

Meanwhile in the world
A scraggly little animal passes
It scurries through the lot
All dust and twigs

And on the television
The one over the gas pumps
Kobe Bryant
Is talking about his father

He is speaking very slowly

And you listen very carefully

Which is when you learn

That the most important thing
                        in this game

                                is to win

                this game

And that this

                Kobe Bryant
Has never forgotten

Now you will feel very confused
You will try to remember your own father

As the animal disappears
        in the scrub brush
                beyond the dumpsters
        and in the sky
                a kind of gloaming
                        is happening

But you don't remember that word
        and you would never say gloaming

And you think again of the vagina
The marvelous vagina
The wrinkled bloom of the labia
The mute pulse of the clit

The night is not a mirror
This night is not the Void
It's a wonderful vagina
You've been standing here for years

MAMMAL ISLAND

Like a ghost
    showing its
first
tender
ghosthood

to another
  quieter
        more
bashful
      ghost

Sunday intrudes

with haze

    and the awkward smell of
Breakfast

It's a floral
and revealing
moment
here between
the dumpsters

The dumpsters
packed with
frozen
LIPS

And beneath this world
they say
there is another

And in that world
another

And beneath that world
there's a tunnel of bees

A bee tunnel of bees

of bee noise
and sleep

But meanwhile: the dread
        And meanwhile: my toes

And all the lists and all the parts

                And all the hopes of every part

And the cohesive ooze of thoughts

on a downhill
careen

        all the way down

rolling rolling
        and up to the hedge
where impaled
    on these leaves
I wiggle and bark

Meanwhile: the haze
        Meanwhile: the tongues

The blood and hair singing

It's a horrible world
and I'm already embarked

And I'm already arrived
I've slept here for real

Is there another a more
horrible world than this one?

Here on Mammal Island
          the slugs
bleed
human milk
          and the world
is a house symbol and
Sacred
          Paper Contingency

                              25 percent more map than land
                    on Mammal Island

Where milk stains all the leaves

And the ponds whirl

And when the light
      comes down
It chimes

INVINCIBILITY

as gasping and helpless as the land

I don't know how this body emits

but I am only LAND RACING

don't let me die

*

and in the next dream I'm working
and in the next dream I'm driving

as gasping and helpless as the sky

grunting in a frozen waste
rock desert
of glass replicas

and in the next dream I'm working

                as a bear exists, grunting
                    in an oozy land-waste

    don't let me die

and in the next dream I'm working

        and in the next dream I'm finding:

one glass drawer

    full of
      one hundred

house replicas

              and in the dark
        public pool:
      a dark
        ribbon
      of blood

and everywhere: car flesh

everyday
car flesh

Invincibility
was the wrong thing
to wish for

and in the next dream I'm talking

and in the next dream I'm working

and gasping, singing, etc.

grunting, knee
grunting

hand grunting

in the next dream I'm
        mouth grunting

sky grunting

                        I don't know how
              this body emits

        and in the next dream I'm washing

AS GASPING AND HELPLESS AS THE SKY

                and in the next dream I'm driving

don't let me die

MORE DREAMS OF WAKING

Terrible dreams of alcohol. Of canals
of alcohol. Of watery transport. Awful
television dreams. Terrible dreams of children.
Reality Children of
Reality Parents. Awful dreams
of children in rows. Of all of us in the bar
as the sun sets on our faces and the
terrible alcohol burns us.
Terrible dreams of houses.
The clouds rush over the houses.
Each cloud with a secret name.
No one will ever know these names.
There are awful dreams of living food.
Terrible dreams of
the Talking Sickness. Of myself
lost in
the transportation. In the
physical translation.
A great bellowing is heard.

Mammalian Howling belies us.
"A bellowing," I say.
I have crossed the parking lot.
I have placed my face
against the building.
I am right here right now.
With terrible dreams of
vehicular clouds, of
bodies locked shut.
But I have come to tell you
of the greater unlocking, of a
type of licking, a type of
licking forth. Of the opening of
eyes, the body of light,
the wind in the trees
and the unnaming of the leaves.
After the Terrible Thought.
After the Dream of the Voice.
After the Death of the Father.
After the Flaming Forth.
I found myself next to a building.
In a kind of parking structure.
There was a great bellowing there.
Was the voice of the city.
The mountains blinked.

The roads lurked.
I was there with you.
After terrible dreams
of the courthouse and law. After the
terrible solemnity of the
robed idiots. After
these dreams we awoke.
We turned off the light.
The fountain slept.
The birds stank.
We sat on a bench.
We died to the world.

IN THE AMERICAN GRAIN

My phone
makes functions
right here
on my fate—

this glare
on the film
on my face.

And this hiss:

some kind
of Abduction—

The faucet

is graceful
and dark

to my cool
flat window
ablaze.
But all this

Augury fails.

I can't
understand
when you lengthen
I can't   understand
  when you look

With urgent
lowercase
pride   the window

gets whiter—
more flat.

Are you done
with ablutions
in prayer?

Right now
I'd sit on your porch

I'd count
the world's

one million
hairs. Oh, the one
million clouds
The wires
partition
that cloud.
"Quiver" goes

fate and the nose.
Attention,
Border Patrol,
edges
from table
       to book:

       Colón
rides high on the deck
   The deck

is slick
with green foam

and he lies about
how many lies—

how many
more miles behind.
One million

invisible sounds

hang out

right under
the ear

My body is here
near the stove.
It's here

in my ankles
and hair.

Colón
alone
patrols
the tall trees

His body
is touching
these trees

My tongue
hangs out
in my face

I heart
his terrible fate

ACKNOWLEDGMENTS

Some of these poems have appeared in the following journals and newspapers: *The Agriculture Reader*; *The Brooklyn Rail*; *Forklift, Ohio*; *H_NGM_N*; and *The Southern California Review*. The author wishes to thank the editors of these publications. He also wishes to thank the following persons whose attention to these poems and this book were of tremendous importance to him: Noelle Kocot, Matt Rohrer, Ellen Sharp, Matthew Zapruder, Maggie Nelson, Joshua Beckman, and Kirsty Singer. Also big thanks are due to Wave Books, Mark Allen and Machine Project, and the School of Critical Studies at the California Institute of the Arts.